Ninja Foodi MAX PRO Health Grill, Flat Plate & Air Fryer Cookbook for Beginners UK

600-Day Quick, Affordable & Tasty Recipes to Grill, Flat Plate, Air Fry, Roast, Bake, Reheat, Dehydrate the Best Meals.

Trevelan Hunt

© Copyright 2022 Trevelan Hunt - All Rights Reserved.

In no way is it legal to reproduce, duplicate, or transmit any part of this document by either electronic means or in printed format. Recording of this publication is strictly prohibited, and any storage of this material is not allowed unless with written permission from the publisher. All rights reserved.

The information provided herein is stated to be truthful and consistent, in that any liability, regarding inattention or otherwise, by any usage or abuse of any policies, processes, or directions contained within is the solitary and complete responsibility of the recipient reader. Under no circumstances will any legal liability or blame be held against the publisher for any reparation, damages, or monetary loss due to the information herein, either directly or indirectly.

Respective authors own all copyrights not held by the publisher.

Legal Notice:

This book is copyright protected. This is only for personal use. You cannot amend, distribute, sell, use, quote or paraphrase any part of the content within this book without the consent of the author or copyright owner. Legal action will be pursued if this is breached.

Disclaimer Notice:

Please note the information contained within this document is for educational and entertainment purposes only. Every attempt has been made to provide accurate, up-to-date and reliable, complete information. No warranties of any kind are expressed or implied. Readers acknowledge that the author is not engaging in the rendering of legal, financial, medical or professional advice.

By reading this document, the reader agrees that under no circumstances are we responsible for any losses, direct or indirect, which are incurred as a result of the use of information contained within this document, including, but not limited to, errors, omissions, or inaccuracies.

Table of Contents

Introduction 5

Chapter 1: Breakfast 15

Chapter 2: Vegetables 22

Chapter 3: Meats 28

Chapter 4: Poultry 40

Chapter 5: Appetizers and Snacks 48

Chapter 6: Fish and Seafood 55

Chapter 7: Desserts 63

Conclusion 71

Appendix recipe Index 72

INTRODUCTION

The top-of-the-line appliance Ninja Foodi MAX PRO Health Grill, Flat Plate & Air Fryer will make preparing meals a breeze. This incredible appliance performs three different types of cooking simultaneously: grill, air fryer, and flat plate cooker. Thanks to this amazing appliance's cutting-edge design and potent performance, you can easily cook all of your favourite dishes.

Utilizing the Ninja Foodi MAX PRO Health Grill, Flat Plate, & Air Fryer, you may become a skilled chef in your own kitchen. You can quickly prepare tasty, healthful meals with this incredible equipment. The air fryer provides your food the ideal crispy finish, while the flat plate grill guarantees even cooking every time.

For your health-conscious lifestyle, the Ninja Foodi MAX PRO Health Grill, Flat Plate, & Air Fryer is the ideal device. It has a flat grill plate for even cooking and an effective air fryer to give your food that crispy finish. Additionally, thanks to its clever design, you can instantly convert between using it as an air fryer or a tabletop grill.

the flat plate and huge grill, which cook perfectly and precisely. Improve your regular cooking with 2 replaceable grill plates: The Powered Grill Plate is ideal for sizzling steaks, pork chops, halloumi skewers, marinated chicken breasts, tuna steaks, and other foods. It offers high heat searing to lock in fluids and produce powerful chargrilled results. To sear and cook delicate foods like prawns, scallops, fajitas, pancakes, eggs, and more, switch to the Flat Plate. Open or shut the cover during cooking.

No guesswork, perfect results with the Smart Cook System. Choose your preferred level of doneness, from rare to well done, and the built-in Digital Cooking Probe will accurately keep track of your food's temperature while it cooks so you don't have to.

With 7 cooking options (Grill, Flat Plate, Air Fry, Roast, Bake, Dehydrate & Reheat), it is more than just a grill. Become an air fryer, which uses up to 75% less fat than deep frying (Tested against deep-fried, hand-cut French fries).

Without the need to flip, cyclonic air technology cooks food rapidly and evenly. From cold to chargrilled, cook. little smoke Grill holds up to 6 burgers and is ideal for 4-6 people. Dishwasher-safe components include a recipe manual written by a chef.

Learning more about your Grill

Function Buttons

Grill: Cooking with a closed lid uses top and bottom heat, making it ideal for grilling large or thick portions of meat, frozen foods, or to sear the entire surface. Cooking with an open lid: Perfect for grilling lean proteins or delicate meals to get chargrilled textures without overcooking.

Roast: vegetables, roast meats, and more.

Air fry: For crispiness and crunch with little to no oil, use air frying.

Bake: Make pastries, treats, cakes, and other things.

Flat Plate: ideal for delicate meals like fish, fajitas, eggs, onions, and eggs.

Reheat: Reviving leftovers with a gentle heat will produce crunchy results.

Dehydrate: For nutritious snacks, dehydrate meats, fruits, and veggies.

Manual: enables you to manually set the internal result with the dial by switching the display.

Preset: You can choose your food type on the display after inserting the probe. To choose your protein, turn the dial.

Cook Level: Select your preferred level of doneness, from rare to well done.

Operating Buttons

Power: Ensure the device is plugged in. Press the button to turn the device on.

Dial: Turn the dial to choose a culinary function or another setting.

Start/Stop: To start or stop the selected cooking function, press the dial's centre.

The appliance enters preheat mode when most cooking functions are initiated; cooking then starts when the temperature setting is met.

Temp: Press the TEMP button to choose the temperature, then use the dial to set it.

Time: Press the TIME button, then use the dial to select the desired cook time.

Function: When the probe is in the "Rest" state (if preheating and cooking have not started), press to clear all settings.

Preheat: When you touch the dial after setting the function, time, and temperature, the appliance will start preheating on its own. When the PREHEAT button is chosen after turning the dial, the preheating process is skipped (not advised).

For Better Results, Preheat Allow the grill to fully warm before adding food for the greatest cooking results. Food that is added before the preheating process is finished may overcook, produce smoke, and take longer to preheat.

The Ninja grills your favourite outside food inside. You can consistently get precisely cooked meat and seafood without any guesswork.

With two interchangeable powered grill plates, discover truly authentic cooking. With the help of a powered grill plate, real chargrilled results are produced. Enjoy thick grill marks and strong scorching. It's ideal for grilling steakhouse-style cuisine, including smoky steaks and pork chops, succulent sausages, marinated chicken breasts, tuna steaks, halloumi skewers, vegetarian kebabs, corn on the cob, and even frozen foods.

Foods that the grill cannot cook are perfect for the flat plate. Thin slices of fish and meat, as well as vegetables, should be seared and sautéed. Salmon, scallops, and prawns can all be prepared with excellent results. In order to harness the high temperature and produce moist and juicy food at any time of day, this smooth plate interlocks with the grill plate.

Additionally, you have the option of cooking with the lid open or closed for greater versatility. Make fried eggs, grilled cheese sandwiches, American pancakes, English breakfasts, and more. Ninja will make the whole family happy.

Ahead of first use

1. Take off all tape, labels, and packaging from the appliance.
2. 2 Take out all the accessories from the box and carefully read this handbook. To prevent any injuries or property damage, please pay close attention to operational directions, warnings, and crucial protections.
3. 3 Grill plate, splatter guard, crisper basket, probe, cleaning brush, and cooking pot should all be washed in warm, soapy water before being properly rinsed and dried. Except for the probe, all accessories are dishwasher safe. NEVER clean the dishwasher's main unit or probe.

Advantage of Your Grill

- Two Adaptable Grill Plates

Grill Plate With Power - This robust grill plate, which is independently powered for direct, edge-to-edge high heat, seals in juices and produces real chargrilled results. Enjoy flavorful results with strong searing and deep grill marks. Whether you love sizzling steaks and pork chops, juicy sausages, seasoned chicken breasts, tuna steaks, halloumi skewers, vegetarian kebabs, chargrilled corn on the cob, or even frozen dishes, this grill is ideal for steakhouse-style grilling. Open or shut the cover during cooking.

Grills cannot cook food on a flat plate. Quickly sear and sauté delicate items; ideal for thinly sliced vegetables and fish and meat dishes like salmon, scallops, prawns, and sirloin steak. To capture the intense heat, the smooth Flat Plate interlocks with the motorised grill plate. A full English morning fry-up, fluffy American pancakes with crispy bacon, fried eggs, grilled cheese sandwiches, burgers, fajitas, stir-fried veggies, teppanyaki-style cookery, and more may now be prepared with the lid open.

- ## No Speculation

What do you think of the steak? Choose your preferred level of doneness, from rare to well done, and Ninja's Smart Cook System will handle the rest!

You don't have to worry about keeping track of the temperature of your meal since the Digital Cooking Probe does it for you! Prepare your preferred cuts of meat and fish to your preferences.

Simply choose a cooking mode and food category from the practical preset options. Choose your preferred level of doneness, from rare to well done, and cook your food with the built-in Digital Cooking Probe. Take your meal outside to rest when the grill beeps; the digital display timer will let you know when it's time to serve.

No speculating. There's no need to be concerned about under or overcooking. Food doesn't need to be cut into to determine readiness. When your meal is ready to be removed and rested before serving, aural signals will let you know.

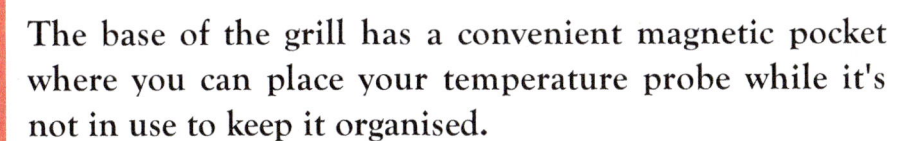

The base of the grill has a convenient magnetic pocket where you can place your temperature probe while it's not in use to keep it organised.

- ## Not a flip grill

Without the need to flip, Cyclonic Air Technology circulates temperatures of up to 260 °C around your food while the lid is closed. Take pleasure in quick, delicious chargrilled results with thorough searing.

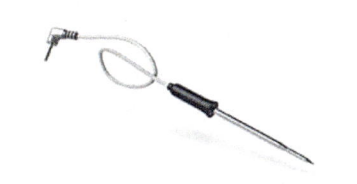

For toppings on everything from loaded nachos to grilled cheese sandwiches, the high-heat airflow that has been collected is ideal for crisping and melting cheese.

- ### Low Smoke

Enhanced flavour, less smoke. A temperature-controlled grill plate and cool-air zone, together with a removable, dishwasher-safe splatter guard, help prevent smoke by keeping the heating element clean.

- ### Beyond a Grill

Use these 7 cooking methods to make delectable entrees, sides, and desserts.

- Grill your favourite outdoor foods inside. Prepare sizzling steaks, burgers, juicy sausages, crispy bacon, spicy marinated chicken breasts, tuna steaks, prawn kebabs, grilled asparagus, corn on the cob, fresh peaches, and more.

- The Flat Plate setting is well suited for cooking gently fajita chicken, peppers and onions, spicy stir fries, bacon and eggs, sriracha-glazed fish, fluffy pancakes, loaded nachos, and even homemade pizza in the traditional method.

- Change into an Air Fryer to cook your favourite fried foods in low-fat versions that contain up to 75% less fat than deep frying. From crunchy broccoli florets and spicy sweet potato wedges to southern-fried chicken goujons.

- Roast succulent pieces of meat or lamb, a spatchcocked bird, root vegetables flavoured with herbs, fluffy roast potatoes, and more.

- Create savory and sweet delicacies by baking everything from chocolate chip cookies to garlic focaccia.

- You can make homemade jerky, dried fruit, vegetable crisps, and even dry herbs by dehydrating fresh ingredients.

- Reheat leftovers to bring back their delectable just-baked flavor; great for pizza, quiche, spring rolls, and more.

Selecting your desired program and selecting between pre-set cooking settings or choosing your own heat with variable temperature controls is simple with a digital display and simple buttons.

4-6 people can be accommodated with a 3.8L Crisper Basket. The huge grill plate has enough space to cook up to 6 hamburgers.

Cook without thawing from frozen to chargrilled.

All removable accessories are non-stick, dishwasher safe, and simple to clean, making clean-up a joy. For simple, convenient storage, all the accessories nest together.

Design of the Ninja Foodi Health Grill & Air Fryer

- Easy-to-use control panel
- Automatic preheating
- Appliance-safe components

The Ninja grill and air fryer measured 11 x 14 x 17 inches/26 x 35.6 x 45 cm, which was larger than we had anticipated (h x w x d). The hinged lid's design also need a substantial amount of leeway around the back for it to fully open. The device feels larger than it actually is since you can't slide it all the way back to the tabletop. Although you can naturally put it back when it's not in use, it still takes up a substantial amount of counter area.

The primary cooking pot has a capacity of 6 quarts (5.7 litres), but if you're air frying, you'll need to add a crisper basket, which reduces the pot's volume to 4 quarts (3.8 litres). Inside the primary cooking pot is a large grill plate that is used for grilling. Although everything can be put in a dishwasher, those without one don't need to worry because a stiff brush is also included to make it easier to clean the grill plate by hand.

Since the grill plate and crisper basket cannot both be placed inside the Ninja Foodi Health Grill & Air Fryer at the same time, you will need room in your cupboard to accommodate both of these components in addition to the gadget itself.

The appliance's front has an easily accessible control panel that is also user-friendly. You can pick from one of four heat settings for grilling. The temperature range for the air fryer is 150-240 °C; for roasting, it is 120-260 °C; and for baking, it is 120-210 °C. It takes longer to cook at lower temperatures (40 90 °C) while using the dehydrate feature. There is no hard setup because of the screen and the simple arrow buttons to change the time and temperature. Even better, the Ninja Foodi Health Grill & Air Fryer automatically preheats and alerts you when your food is ready to be added. However, it doesn't prompt you to shake or stir during air frying.

There is a tonne of advice on choosing the right time and temperature for cooking typical items in a quick-start guide and a recipe book with cooking charts. However, keep in mind that there aren't many suggestions for the roast and bake functions, so you'll need to experiment with them.

Performance of the Ninja Foodi Health Grill & Air Fryer

- When air frying, have enough of room to spread out the food.
- Grill bar marks are curved rather than straight.
- Foods brown and cook uniformly

It's a little bit unusual to use this air fryer than a typical one with a pull-out basket. Here, the crisper basket is instead designed to slide into the appliance; to retrieve the food, simply raise the top lid. The setup is the same as other air fryers; however, it can be more difficult to shake food while it is cooking because you need to remove the hot crisper basket.

We prepared a batch of frozen thick-cut fries to cook in the air fryer to evaluate its functionality. We allowed the cooker to heat up while the crisper basket was inside at 180 °C. It took three minutes to complete. The Ninja Foodi Health Grill & Air Fryer encouraged us to add the food when it heated up and immediately began the countdown timer when the lid was closed. Although there isn't a warning to shake or turn food when air frying, we checked it halfway through by removing the basket with oven gloves and shaking the fries. The resulting fries were crisp, golden, and perfectly cooked after 20 minutes. In addition to tasting fantastic, they also finished cooking in less time than the 28 minutes they would have needed in an oven.

After that, we air-fried chicken wings. We were impressed to see that the basket had room for seven wings to sit side by side, with plenty of room to spare for stacking additional wings. We prepared the wings for air frying by coating them in 12 tbsp oil and preheating the air fryer to 200 °C. After 10 minutes, we rotated the wings, and 15 minutes later, the flesh was moist and soft and the skin was gorgeously golden.

We evaluated the Ninja Foodi Health Grill & Air Fryer's capacity to cook raw hand-cut fries in our third test. We submerged the raw fries in cold water for 30 minutes as instructed by the air fry chart, and then thoroughly dry them. We dipped them in 1 tablespoon of oil and warmed the air fryer to 200 °C. We gave them a shake after 10 and 15 minutes of cooking, which is the recommended cooking time on the chart of 23 to 26 minutes. After 18 minutes, we took them out because they were cooked and beautifully brown. The exterior of the fry was evenly crisped and browned while the interior was fluffy.

Since grilling is one of the main uses for this air fryer, we gave it a try by grilling two beef patties. We turned the grill to high for 6 minutes as directed per the grilling chart. It takes around 8 minutes for the grill to heat up, and you have to make sure the grill plate is inside so it will be hot when the food is added. We placed the patties in the hot pan, cooked them for three minutes, and then rotated them. The Ninja's little smoke and cooking scent emissions really amazed us. The burgers were well-done and had charred lines on the outside, however, due to the form of the grill plate's bars, the markings were curved rather than the expected straight lines.

Because of the non-stick coating, cleaning the cooking pot and basket is simple. You could also put them in the dishwasher.. The grill plate requires a little more finesse to wash by hand, but Ninja's brush makes it simpler.

On our noise meter, the grill barely hit 58dB, which isn't at all excessively loud, while the air fryer didn't exceed 55dB at all.

How To Clean Your Grill

After each usage, the appliance needs to be completely cleaned. Before cleaning, always allow the equipment to cool.

- Before cleaning, unplug the appliance from the wall socket. After removing your food, leave the lid open to help the appliance cool more rapidly.
- All supplied accessories, with the exception of the probe, are dishwasher safe: the cooking pot, grill plate, crisper basket, splatter shield, cleaning brush, and any additional accessories.
- The probe MUST NOT be put in the dishwasher.
- Before putting the grill plate, crisper basket, splatter guard, and any other accessories in the dishwasher, we advise giving them a warm water rinse for the best dishwasher cleaning results.
- If washing by hand, we advise washing the parts with the provided cleaning brush. To help remove cheese or sauce that has baked on, use the cleaning brush's opposite end as a scraper. After hand washing, let all portions air dry or towel dry.
- Soak in warm, soapy water before cleaning if food particles or grease are attached to the grill plate, splatter guard, or any other removable element.
- After each usage, clean the splatter guard.
- The grease that has been baked on can be loosened by soaking the splatter guard overnight. After soaking, use the cleaning brush to scrub away the grease from the front tabs and stainless steel frame.
- Boil the splatter guard in a pot of water for ten minutes to thoroughly clean it. After that, rinse with warm water and let everything air dry fully.
- Soak the silicone grip and stainless steel tip of the probe in warm, soapy water to thoroughly clean it. The cord or jack MUST NOT be submerged in water or any other liquid.
- Only hand wash the probe storage chamber holder.

Chapter 1: Breakfast

Grilled Pesto Tomatoes on Toast

Prep Time: 4 Mins
Cook Time: 5 Mins   Serves: 1

Ingredients:

- 2 medium tomatoes
- 1 tbsp pesto sauce
- a slice country-style bread

Directions:

1. Halve the tomatoes. Thin the pesto sauce with a little water and brush half on the tomatoes. Cook under a hot grill for 5-7 mins until softened. At the same time, toast the slice of bread, then spread with the remaining pesto mix. Top with the hot tomatoes, squashing them slightly.

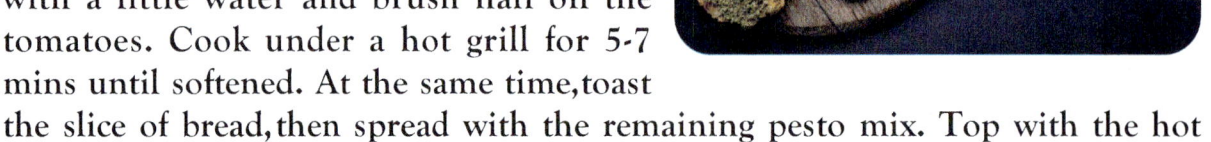

Nutritional Value (Amount per Serving):

Calories: 185; Fat: 11.65; Carb: 10.29; Protein: 11.6

Spiced Flat Breads

Prep Time: 35 Mins
Cook Time: 10 Mins   Serves: 8

Ingredients:

- 140g plain flour
- 140g wholemeal flour
- 7g sachet easy-blend yeast
- 1 tbsp melted butter, plus extra for brushing
- or the quick spice paste (optional)
- 2 fat garlic cloves, chopped
- 1 large red or green chilli, seeded and chopped
- 2 tsp sesame seeds
- 2 tsp ground fenugreek or ground coriander
- 2 tbsp olive oil
- 2 tbsp chopped coriander

Directions:

1. If making the paste, use a food processor, electric spice mill or pestle and mortar

to blend together the garlic, chilli, sesame seeds and ground spice to a thick paste. Work in the oil, then the coriander, to a spreading paste and season. Set aside.

2. Put the flours, 1 tsp salt and yeast into a large bowl and mix. Stir 120ml tepid water into the melted butter, then mix this into the flour, adding extra drops of tepid water until you have a smooth dough. Knead on a lightly floured surface for 5 mins, then return to the bowl, cover and leave in a warm place to rise until doubled in size. This should take 1 hr.

3. Divide the dough into 8 balls. Roll out each ball on a lightly floured surface to a rough 18cm circle the thickness of a 10p coin. Prick each one well with a fork to stop them rising. To cook on a barbecue: put the breads on the centre of the grill. Cook for a few mins, then turn and cook the other side. If using the paste, spread 1 tsp on one side as the breads come off the heat. Otherwise, brush the breads with more melted butter. Reheat the griddle between batches and stack them on top of each other to keep warm.

Nutritional Value (Amount per Serving):

Calories: 253; Fat: 7.87; Carb: 28.35; Protein: 16.8

Cheesy French Toast With Ham Grilled Vine Tomatoes

Prep Time: 10 Mins
Cook Time: 20 Mins   Serves: 6

Ingredients:

- 5 eggs, beaten
- 4 tbsp milk
- 140g gruyre, grated
- 1 tbsp chopped chives
- knob of butter
- 1large baguette, thickly sliced
- 250g cherry tomatoes on the vine
- olive oil, for grilling
- 250g sliced ham - about 25 slices (James used Serrano)
- watercress, to serve

Directions:

1. Heat the grill to high. In a shallow bowl, whisk together the eggs, milk, cheese and chives. Melt the butter in a large non-stick pan over a medium heat. Dip slices of bread into the egg mixture, then place them in the pan. Cook for 3-5 mins on each side, or until golden and crisp, then keep warm in a low oven if you need to.

2. Place the vine tomatoes on a baking tray, drizzle with a little oil and season with salt and pepper. Grill until they start to soften and blister. On a large platter, pile up the cheesy French bread, grilled tomatoes, sliced ham and a pile of watercress,

and let everyone dig in.

Nutritional Value (Amount per Serving):

Calories: 618; Fat: 54.36; Carb: 11.92; Protein: 21.99

Hoisin Hot Dogs

Prep Time: 15 Mins
Cook Time: 20 Mins   Serves: 4

Ingredients:

- 1 tbsp sriracha
- 1 tbsp mayonnaise
- 4 sausages
- 2 tbsp hoisin sauce
- 4 brioche hot dog buns
- 1/4 thinly sliced cucumber
- 4 sliced spring onions

Directions:

1. Mix the sriracha with the mayonnaise. Brush the sausages with the hoisin sauce and cook under a grill following pack instructions. Split the hot dog buns, fill each with a sausage and spoon over some extra hoisin sauce. Top with the cucumber, the sriracha mayonnaise and spring onions.

Nutritional Value (Amount per Serving):

Calories: 149; Fat: 9.37; Carb: 9.97; Protein: 8.53

Breakfast Muffin

Prep Time: 5 Mins
Cook Time: 20 Mins   Serves: 4

Ingredients:

- 400g good quality
- pork sausages
- 10g panko breadcrumbs
- 1 tsp dried mixed herbs
- Vegetable spray oil
- 4 eggs
- 1 tsp white wine vinegar
- 4 breakfast muffins, halved
- 2 tbsps tomato ketchup

Directions:

1. Using a sharp knife, cut through the sausage skin, remove and discard. Put the sausage meat in a bowl with the panko breadcrumbs and mixed herbs. Using your hands, combine the ingredients then shape into four even sized patties, pressing them down until they are slightly larger than the muffins.
2. Spray the sausage patties on both sides with oil and insert the 10-in-1 wire rack into the air fryer with the grill plate, flat side up, on top of the wire rack. Set the temperature to 180 °C and preheat the grill plate for 3 minutes. Carefully add the sausage patties to the grill and cook for 12-15 minutes, turning halfway through.
3. Carefully remove the rack and grill plate out of the airfryer and put onto a heat proof surface. Wear oven gloves to remove the wire rack and grill plate from the airfryer as they will be very hot. Transfer the patties to a plate and cover with foil to keep warm.
4. Meanwhile bring a pan of water to the boil, add the vinegar and crack the egg into a small bowl. Give the water a stir to create a whirlpool effect, then pour the egg into the water, repeat quickly with the remaining eggs. Cook the eggs for 4 minutes, then transfer to a plate lined with kitchen paper using a slotted spoon.
5. Whilst the eggs cook, set the air fryer temperature to 200 °C and place the breakfast muffins onto the wire toasting rack, making sure that they are evenly spaced. Toast for 4-5 minutes, until the muffins are lightly toasted and warmed.
6. To assemble, place a sausage pattie on each muffin base, top with a poached egg and finish with a muffin lid. Serve with ketchup on the side.

Nutritional Value (Amount per Serving):

Calories: 303; Fat: 18.5; Carb: 11.96; Protein: 21.

Air Fryer Chickpeas

Prep Time: 2 Mins
Cook Time: 15 Mins   Serves: 1

Ingredients:

- 1 x 400g tin chickpeas, drained and rinsed
- 1 tbsp olive oil
- 2 tsp spice or herb seasoning

Directions:

1. Drain and rinse the chickpeas.
2. Add the oil and your choice of spices or herbs (see notes).
3. Toss the chickpeas until they are coated in the oil and seasoning.

4. Transfer to the crisper basket and set off at 200 °C, and air fry for 15 minutes, shaking two or three times.
5. The chickpeas should be hard and crispy when they are ready. If they are still a little soft, air fry them for a few more minutes. Add extra seasoning if required.

Nutritional Value (Amount per Serving):

Calories: 139; Fat: 13.52; Carb: 3.53; Protein: 0.33

Air Fryer Breakfast Potatoes

Prep Time: 10 Mins
Cook Time: 15 Mins   Serves: 2

Ingredients:

- 2 x medium/large potatoes
- 1 tbsp olive oil
- 1/2 tsp smoked paprika
- 1/2 tsp black pepper
- 1/2 tsp garlic salt

Directions:

1. Peel and chop potatoes into 1-inch cubes. Use approximately 1 medium to large potato per serving.
2. Preheat the air fryer to 200 °C for about 5 minutes
3. Rinse chopped potatoes in water and pat dry with kitchen towel.
4. Coat potatoes in oil and sprinkle seasoning over them. Stir so that they are all covered.
5. Transfer potatoes to crisper basket and cook for 15 minutes. Check on them at the halfway mark and give them a shake. Depending on your air fryer make they might take less or more time so keep an eye on them when you first cook them. They are ready when they are golden brown and crispy.

Nutritional Value (Amount per Serving):

Calories: 348; Fat: 7.19; Carb: 65.5; Protein: 7.66

Air Fryer Jacket Potato

Prep Time: 5 Mins
Cook Time: 20 Mins   Serves: 2

Ingredients:

- 1 Large baking potato
- 1/2 Tablespoon olive oil
- Salt and pepper
- Optional toppings: butter,cheese,beans,tuna, etc.

Directions:

1. Preheat your air fryer to 200 °C.
2. While the air fryer is warming up,wash your potato and slice it in half lengthwise.
3. Rub the potato halves with olive oil and season with salt and pepper.
4. Place the potato halves in the crisper basket and cook at 200 °C for 20 minutes.
5. Remove from the air fryer and add your desired toppings. Serve immediately. Enjoy!

Nutritional Value (Amount per Serving):

Calories: 189; Fat: 5.6; Carb: 31.52; Protein: 3.79

Chapter 2: Vegetables

Quinoa Salad With Grilled Halloumi

Prep Time: 15 Mins
Cook Time: 25 Mins   Serves: 3

Ingredients:

- 3 tbsp extra-virgin olive oil
- 1 small red onion ,sliced
- 1 large roasted pepper from a jar, thickly sliced, or a handful of ready-roasted sliced peppers
- 200g quinoa
- 500ml vegetable stock
- small bunch flat-leaf parsley , roughly chopped
- zest and juice 1 lemon
- large pinch sugar
- 250g pack halloumi cheese ,cut into 6 sliced

Directions:

1. Heat 1 tbsp of the oil in a medium saucepan. Cook the onion and pepper for a few mins, then add the quinoa and cook for a further 3 mins. Add the stock, cover and turn the heat down to a simmer. Cook for 15 mins or until soft, then stir through half the parsley. Heat the grill.
2. Meanwhile, mix the lemon zest and juice with the remaining parsley and oil, and a large pinch of sugar and salt. Grill the halloumi until both sides are golden and crisp. Serve the salad with the grilled halloumi and the dressing poured over everything.

Nutritional Value (Amount per Serving):

Calories: 2107; Fat: 205.15; Carb: 51.35; Protein: 30.88

Crispy Grilled Feta With Saucy Butter Beans

Prep Time: 2 Mins
Cook Time: 18 Mins   Serves: 4

Ingredients:

- 500ml passata
- 2 x 400g cans butter beans ,drained and rinsed
- 2 garlic cloves ,crushed

- 1 tsp dried oregano, plus a pinch
- 200g spinach
- 2 roasted red peppers, sliced
- 1/2 lemon, zested and juiced
- 100g block of feta, cut into chunks
- 1/2 tsp olive oil
- 4 small pittas

Directions:

1. Put a large ovenproof frying pan over a medium-high heat, and tip in the passata, butter beans, garlic, oregano, spinach and peppers. Stir together and cook for 6-8 mins until the sauce is bubbling and the spinach has wilted. Season, then add the lemon juice.
2. Heat the grill to high. Scatter the feta over the sauce, so it's still exposed, drizzle with the olive oil and sprinkle over the lemon zest plus a pinch of oregano, then grind over some black pepper. Grill for 5-8 mins until the feta is golden and crisp at the edges.
3. Meanwhile, toast the pittas under the grill or in the toaster, then serve with the beans and feta.

Nutritional Value (Amount per Serving):

Calories: 179; Fat: 5.47; Carb: 24.49; Protein: 10.32

Grilled Courgette, Bean Cheese Quesadilla

Prep Time: 10 Mins
Cook Time: 20 Mins   Serves: 4

Ingredients:

- 1 onion, finely chopped
- 4 tsp olive oil
- 4 garlic cloves, finely chopped
- 2 tsp ground cumin
- 1 tbsp tomato purée
- 400g can pinto bean, drained and rinsed
- 3 courgettes, sliced on the diagonal
- 175g cheddar, grated
- 1 green chilli, finely chopped
- large handful coriander, roughly chopped
- 8 flour tortillas

Directions:

1. Fry the onion in half the olive oil for about 5 mins or until soft. Stir through the garlic and cumin. Cook over a low heat for 1 min more. Add the tomato purée, pinto beans and a few tbsp of water. Heat through, then mash up with the back of a fork and season.

2. Meanwhile, toss the courgette slices in the remaining oil with some seasoning. Place on a hot griddle pan and cook for a couple of mins each side until tender and grill marked. Place to one side.
3. Mix the cheese, chilli and coriander in a bowl. Spread the bean purée over half of the tortillas. Lay over courgette slices and scatter with cheese mixture. Top with the remaining tortillas, pressing the two together. Cook in batches in the hot griddle pan, carefully turning, for about 1-2 mins each side or until the cheese has begun to melt and the tortillas are crisp. Serve in wedges.

Nutritional Value (Amount per Serving):

Calories: 827; Fat: 32.93; Carb: 97.39; Protein: 39.18

Grilled Aubergines With Spicy Chickpeas Walnut Sauce

Prep Time: 20 Mins
Cook Time: 30 Mins   Serves: 2

Ingredients:

- 4 tbsp olive oil
- 1 onion, finely chopped
- 1 red chilli, deseeded and finely chopped
- 2cm piece ginger, finely chopped
- 1/2tsp each ground cumin, coriander and cinnamon
- 400g can chickpeas, rinsed and drained
- 200g tomatoes, chopped
- juice 1/2 lemon
- 2 aubergines, sliced lengthways
- or The Walnut Sauce
- 200g tub Greek-style yogurt
- handful coriander leaves, roughly chopped
- 1 garlic clove, crushed
- 25g walnuts, chopped

Directions:

1. Heat 2 tbsp oil in a pan, add the onion and fry until soft and lightly browned, about 10 mins. Add the chilli, ginger and spices and mix well. Stir in the chickpeas, tomatoes and 5 tbsp water, bring to the boil, then simmer for 10 mins. Add a little salt and pepper and the lemon juice.
2. Arrange the aubergines over a grill pan. Brush lightly with oil, sprinkle with salt and pepper, then grill until golden. Flip them over, brush again with oil, season and grill again until tender and golden.
3. Mix the yogurt with the garlic, most of the walnuts and coriander and a little salt and pepper. Arrange the aubergine slices over a warm platter and spoon over the chickpea mix. Drizzle with the walnut sauce and scatter with the remaining

walnuts and coriander.

Nutritional Value (Amount per Serving):

Calories: 958; Fat: 57.22; Carb: 79.17; Protein: 39.22

Grilled Mediterranean Veg With Bean Mash

Prep Time: 15 Mins
Cook Time: 25 Mins   Serves: 2

Ingredients:

- 1 red pepper ,deseeded and quartered
- 1 aubergine ,sliced lengthways
- 2 courgettes ,sliced lengthways
- 2 tbsp olive oil
- or The Mash
- 410g can haricot bean ,rinsed
- 1 garlic clove ,crushed
- 100ml vegetable stock
- 1 tbsp chopped coriander
- lemon wedges,to serve

Directions:

1. Heat the grill. Arrange the vegetables over a grill pan and brush lightly with oil. Grill until lightly browned, turn them over, brush again with oil, then grill until tender.
2. Meanwhile, put the beans in a small pan with the garlic and stock. Bring to the boil, then simmer, uncovered, for 10 mins. Mash roughly with a potato masher, adding a little water or more stock if the mash seems too dry. Divide the veg and mash between 2 plates, drizzle over any leftover oil and sprinkle with black pepper and coriander. Add a lemon wedge to each plate and serve.

Nutritional Value (Amount per Serving):

Calories: 1153; Fat: 96.34; Carb: 13.48; Protein: 66.44

Stuffed Grilled Vegetable Bites

Prep Time: 15 Mins
Cook Time: 35 Mins   Serves: 8

Ingredients:

- 1 large aubergine (about 350g/12oz)
- 1 large courgette (about 300g/11oz)
- 2 flame-roasted peppers, from a jar
- 1 garlic clove, crushed
- 3 tbsp olive oil
- 250g tub ricotta
- 25g finely grated parmesan (or vegetarian alternative)
- 3 sundried or semi-dried tomatoes in oil (from a jar), drained and finely chopped
- finely grated zest 0.5 lemon
- 8 basil leaves
- small handful parsley, leaves picked and roughly chopped
- 1/2tsp paprika

Directions:

1. Cut the aubergine and courgette into thin lengths about 2-3mm thick – you should have 8 slices of each. Drain and rinse the peppers, remove any seeds, pat dry, then cut into quarters. Mix the garlic with the olive oil and some seasoning.
2. Heat the grill plate over a medium heat. Brush the vegetable slices with the garlic oil and cook for 2-3 mins each side until completely soft and lightly charred (you'll need to do this in batches) Set aside on a plate and leave to cool. The vegetables can be griddled the day before and kept covered in the fridge – bring to room temperature before serving.
3. Mix together the cheeses, sundried tomatoes, lemon zest and seasoning. Lay out the slices of aubergine on a large board. Top each with a slice of courgette, a strip of pepper, and a basil leaf. Dot 1 tbsp of the cheese mix on top and roll the vegetables up. Skewer with a cocktail stick to secure.
4. When ready to serve, arrange on a plate and scatter over the parsley leaves and paprika.

Nutritional Value (Amount per Serving):

Calories: 185; Fat: 18.4; Carb: 4.29; Protein: 1.95

Chapter 3: Meats

Air Fryer Beef Wellington

Prep Time: 15 Mins
Cook Time: 1 Hr 19 Mins   Serves: 6

Ingredients:

- arlic Mushrooms Ingredients
- 250 g Mushrooms
- Extra Virgin Olive Oil Spray
- Fresh Rosemary
- 6 Garlic Cloves
- 1 Tsp Garlic Powder
- Salt & Pepper
- 1 Tbsp Butter
- eef Wellington Ingredients (Make Ahead)
- 1 Kg Beef Fillet
- Extra Virgin Olive Oil Spray
- 2 Tsp Thyme
- 2 Tsp Parsley
- Salt & Pepper
- eef Wellington Ingredients (Next Day)
- 1 kg Frozen Puff Pastry
- 200 g Brussels Pate
- Egg Wash

Directions:

1. Slice mushrooms into thirds (lengthways) and place them into the crisper basket. Spray with extra virgin olive oil and season with salt, pepper, and garlic powder. Then find room in the air fryer basket for some fresh rosemary and some peeled garlic cloves.
2. Air fry for 9 minutes at 180 °C and you will have a wonderful garlic and rosemary aroma in your kitchen.
3. Discard the rosemary and remove the mushrooms and load into a bowl that you have added almost melted butter to. Then make sure the mushrooms and garlic are well coated in the butter. Then load into the fridge for tomorrow.
4. Place your fillet steak on a chopping board, score and then add extra virgin olive oil, salt, pepper, thyme, and parsley.
5. Air fry your steak for 5 minutes at 180 °C, turn over and then do another 5 minutes on the same temp on the other side.
6. Allow the fillet to rest until cool, then get rid of any excess juices and wrap in foil and fridge overnight.
7. The next day allow the fillet, the pate, the mushrooms, and the puff pastry to go to room temperature.
8. Roll out your pastry and spread on a layer of your pate. Then add a layer of mushrooms. Making sure you have enough mushrooms and pate for the top

layer.
9. Then add your beef over the pate and mushrooms.
10. Next repeat step 8 again for your pastry layer that is going on top. Though note, you don't need the pastry as big for the top section.
11. Then place the top of the pastry over the beef wellington.
12. Now add a layer of egg wash so that the pastry top and bottom will stick together and then tightly seal up the pastry.
13. Turn over the beef wellington and now use scissors or a knife to do two cuts in the top for the wellington to breathe.
14. Then add a layer of egg wash before placing in the air fryer basket.
15. Air fry for 50 minutes at 180 °C for a medium rare or 60 minutes for a medium to well.
16. Allow to rest for 5 minutes (note it carries on cooking then) and then slice and serve.

Nutritional Value (Amount per Serving):

Calories: 1291; Fat: 93.58; Carb: 86.49; Protein: 26.98

Homemade Air Fryer Fishcakes

Prep Time: 10 Mins
Cook Time: 35 Mins   Serves: 4

Ingredients:

- ook The Fish
- 1 Pink Salmon Fillet
- 1 Cod Fillet
- 1 Pollock Fillet
- 2 Tsp Dill
- Salt & Pepper
- ook The Potatoes
- 300 g Baby Potatoes
- 2 Tsp Extra Virgin Olive Oil
- 2 Tsp Butter
- ake The Production Line
- 2 Eggs beaten
- 480 ml Breadcrumbs
- 480 ml Plain Flour/All Purpose
- 2 Tbsp Lemon Juice
- 1 Tbsp Parsley
- 2 Tsp Dill Tops
- 2 Tsp Parsley
- Salt & Pepper
- 2 Tsp Basil
- Salt & Pepper
- ake The Fishcakes
- 2 Tsp Coriander
- 2 Tsp Thai 7 Spice
- 2 Tsp Sweet Paprika
- 1 Tbsp Fresh Parsley shredded
- Salt & Pepper
- 1 Tbsp Butter

Directions:

1. Place your mixed fish fillets in a bowl and let them sit for an hour to get rid of any excess liquid. If they are frozen, you can defrost them in the bowl first.
2. Then remove the fish (minus the excess water) and place on a chopping board. Season well with salt, pepper, and dill. Load the fish into the air fryer and cook for 8 minutes at 180 °C then place in bowl and use a fork to flake the fish.
3. In another bowl add baby potatoes, extra virgin olive oil and salt and pepper. Mix with your hands for an even coat. Air fry for 17 minutes at 180c and then mash with a little butter. Add the mash to the cooked fish, and then add the fishcake seasoning list.
4. Use a fork or a masher to mash well and then once cool enough to touch make into Thai fish patties.
5. Though whilst you are waiting for them to cool set up your production line. Beaten egg in one bowl with lemon juice, flour and the 1tbsp of parsley in another bowl and the breadcrumbs and the rest of the seasoning in a third. Make sure all bowls are well mixed and that they are in the order of flour, egg, breadcrumbs.
6. Once you have made your Thai fish cakes load into the flour, into the egg and the breadcrumbs getting a good coating from each.
7. Load into the air fryer basket and air fry for 10 minutes at 180 °C or until fully heated through and you have a crispy breadcrumb texture.

Nutritional Value (Amount per Serving):

Calories: 1142; Fat: 22.67; Carb: 172.17; Protein: 58.9

Air Fryer Roast Beef

Prep Time: 5 Mins
Cook Time: 45 Mins   Serves: 4

Ingredients:

- easoning
- 2 tsp coarse salt
- 1 tsp freshly ground black pepper
- 1/2tsp dried thyme
- 1/2tsp garlic granules
- 1/2tsp dried rosemary
- 1/2tsp mustard powder or brown sugar
- or The Roast Beef
- 1.2 kg roasting beef joint check it fits into your Air fryer
- 3 tbsp olive oil

Directions:

1. Take your beef joint out of the fridge and pat dry. Leave it to come to room temperature for 30 minutes. Make sure to check whether your joint fits into the air fryer. You can always slice a larger joint in half.
2. Meanwhile, preheat the air fryer 200 °C for 10 minutes. Mix all the seasoning ingredients together and brush the beef all over with olive oil. Press the seasoning mix all over the beef.
3. Use a liner in the crisper basket (optional) and position the beef on top. Roast for 10-15 minutes. Cooking the beef at a high temperature will create a lovely crust on the exterior, sealing all the lovely juices within in the same way that searing the beef in a skillet before roasting in the oven.
4. Remove the crisper basket and turn the beef over. Reduce the temperature to 180 °C and cook for a further 30 minutes.
5. Start checking the internal temperature of the beef with an instant read thermometer inserting the probe in the middle thickest part. Use the table in the recipe notes as a guide to cook it to your liking, adding five minutes of cooking time until your preferred temperature is reached. Remember that the temperature of the joint will continue to rise slightly as it rests so factor that in. I usually aim for medium rare (55-57 °C).
6. Once the beef is cooked to your liking place it on a warm platter and cover loosely with foil. Leave it to rest for 20-30 minutes before slicing against the grain and serving with your favorite side dishes.

Nutritional Value (Amount per Serving):

Calories: 679; Fat: 37.6; Carb: 3.49; Protein: 76.75

Grilled Steak Topped With Ceps

Prep Time: 20 Mins
Cook Time: 20 Mins   Serves: 2

Ingredients:

- 1 tbsp olive oil
- 2 sirloin steaks, about 140g/5oz each
- or The Topping
- 25g butter
- 100g fresh ceps, trimmed and finely sliced
- 1 garlic clove, chopped
- 50ml white wine
- small handful mixed soft herbs such as parsley, chives and tarragon, leaves picked and finely chopped
- 1 tbsp crème fraîche
- 1 egg yolk
- 25g parmesan, grated

Directions:

1. First, make the topping. Heat the butter in a frying pan until foaming, then fry the ceps for 4 mins until soft. Add the garlic, cook for 1 min more, then splash the wine into the pan and simmer until dry. Tip the ceps into a bowl and combine with the rest of the ingredients.
2. Heat the grill to high. Heat the oil in a large frying pan until practically smoking, then sear the steaks for 1 min on each side until well browned (this will give you a rare steak). Spoon the topping over the steaks and place under the grill for 3-4 mins until bubbling and golden. Lift the steaks onto plates and serve with salad.

Nutritional Value (Amount per Serving):

Calories: 385; Fat: 30.8; Carb: 10.09; Protein: 17.4

Grilled Pork With Lemon Thyme Barley

Prep Time: 10 Mins
Cook Time: 40 Mins   Serves: 4

Ingredients:

- 4 pork medallions
- 2 tbsp red wine vinegar
- 2 garlic cloves, crushed
- 1 tbsp sunflower oil
- 1 small onion, finely chopped
- 1 tsp coriander seeds   • 200g pearl barley
- 600ml hot chicken stock
- 4 lemon thyme sprigs, leaves only
- 100g bag baby spinach • juice and zest 1 lemon

Directions:

1. Place the pork in a shallow dish and add the vinegar and garlic, turning to make sure they're evenly covered. Leave at room temperature for 10 mins. Meanwhile, heat the oil in a pan and cook the onion and coriander seeds for 3-4 mins until softened.
2. Add the barley and cook for 1 min in the oil, then add the stock and thyme. Bring to the boil, cover then simmer for 30-35 mins until the barley is tender and the liquid absorbed.
3. Transfer the pork to a grill plate and cook under a hot grill for 5 mins on each side until nicely browned and cooked through. Stir the spinach, zest and juice into the barley and spoon onto plates. Serve with the grilled pork.

Nutritional Value (Amount per Serving):

Calories: 898; Fat: 41.2; Carb: 46.31; Protein: 83.1

Grilled Steak Salad With Horseradish Dressing

Prep Time: 10 Mins
Cook Time: 5 Mins   Serves: 2

Ingredients:

- 250g/9oz bavette or skirt steak
- 1 tsp celery seeds, crushed
- 1 tbsp Worcestershire sauce
- little olive oil, for brushing
- 6 celery sticks, thinly sliced, leaves reserved
- 200g mixed tomato, sliced or halved (beefsteak, plum and red and yellow cherry are all good)
- or the dressing
- 1 tbsp Worcestershire sauce
- 1 tbsp olive oil
- 1 tsp horseradish sauce
- 1 tsp red wine vinegar
- 1 tsp tomato purée

Directions:

1. Rub the steak on both sides with the crushed celery seeds, some seasoning and the Worcestershire sauce. Brush with olive oil and leave to marinate while you prepare the salad.
2. Mix the dressing ingredients in a small bowl. Divide the celery and tomatoes between 2 plates. Heat the grill plate over a high heat, then cook the meat for 2-3 mins on each side (depending on how thick your steaks are). Remove from the heat and leave to rest, covered with foil, for 5 mins.
3. Slice the steaks and place on top of the salads, pour the dressing over and scatter over the celery leaves.

Nutritional Value (Amount per Serving):

Calories: 1043; Fat: 83.88; Carb: 9.37; Protein: 62.13

Pork Chop Melts

Prep Time: 10 Mins
Cook Time: 20 Mins   Serves: 4

Ingredients:

- 4 pork chops ,about 175g/6oz each
- 100-140g stilton or other blue cheese such as bleu d'Auvergne or Danish Blue
- 4 rounded tbsp apple sauce
- mashed potato and green veg,to serve

Directions:

1. Turn on the grill. Season the chops on both sides with a good sprinkling of salt and pepper. Grill under a moderate heat for 12-16 minutes,turning once,until just cooked.
2. Add the topping. Thinly slice the cheese (don't worry if it breaks up a bit). Spoon the apple sauce over the chops and top each one with a couple of slices of cheese. Slide back under the grill for 2-3 minutes until the cheese is melted and tinged brown. Serve with mashed potatoes and a green veg such as leeks or broccoli,and with any melted cheesy bits from the bottom of the pan.

Nutritional Value (Amount per Serving):

Calories: 66; Fat: 1.75; Carb: 10.44; Protein: 2.69

Grilled Saigon Pork Rib

Prep Time: 25 Mins
Cook Time: 1 Hr   Serves: 4

Ingredients:

- 8 baby back pork ribs,separated
- 30g yellow bean or miso paste
- 10g ginger ,peeled and sliced
- 2 star anise
- 2 cardamom pods ,lightly bashed
- 1 tbsp rice vinegar
- 50g rock or granulated sugar
- 3 tbsp honey
- or the sauce
- 150g rock or granulated sugar

- 65ml fish sauce
- 1/2 green chilli ,finely chopped
- 1/2 red chilli ,finely chopped
- 1/4 tsp ground black pepper
- o serve
- 2 carrots ,cut into ribbons using a vegetable peeler
- pickled mooli (optional)
- 30g roasted unsalted peanuts ,finely chopped
- 10g sesame seeds
- a few dill sprigs

Directions:

1. Grill the ribs on high for 10 mins, then put them in a saucepan with 1 1/2 litres water, the bean or miso paste, ginger, star anise, cardamom, rice vinegar, sugar and 1 tsp sea salt. Bring to a simmer, cover and cook over a very low heat for 20 mins.
2. Meanwhile, make the sauce. Put 150ml water in a saucepan and bring to a rolling boil. Add the sugar, lower the heat and stir until completely dissolved. Allow the sugar syrup to cool, then blend with the fish sauce, chillies and black pepper.
3. Remove the ribs from the pan and spread evenly with the honey. Grill the ribs on high for 12 mins, turning halfway through. Mix the pork ribs with the sauce.

Nutritional Value (Amount per Serving):

Calories: 996; Fat: 35.89; Carb: 73.3; Protein: 92.59

Sesame Beef Skewers With Cucumber Salad

Prep Time: 10 Mins
Cook Time: 6 Mins   Serves: 4

Ingredients:

- 4 thin-cut sirloin steaks or minute steaks, trimmed of any fat and each cut into 3 long strips
- 100ml sachet stir-fry sauce (we used oyster and spring onion)
- 1 tbsp sesame seeds
- or the salad
- 1 tsp white wine vinegar
- 1 tsp light soy sauce
- 1 cucumber ,cut into small chunks
- 3 spring onions ,sliced
- 1/2 red chilli ,deseeded and finely chopped
- handful coriander leaves, chopped

Directions:

1. Heat grill to high. In a bowl, mix the steak strips with the stir-fry sauce and sesame seeds. Thread onto 12 skewers, then grill for 12 mins, turning halfway

through, until golden and sticky.
2. For the salad, mix the vinegar and soy together, then toss with the cucumber, spring onions, chilli and coriander. Serve with the beef skewers and some boiled basmati rice.

Nutritional Value (Amount per Serving):

Calories: 1167; Fat: 68.94; Carb: 3.8; Protein: 124.75

Leek Sage Risotto With Grilled Crisp Bacon

Prep Time: 10 Mins
Cook Time: 20 Mins   Serves: 1

Ingredients:

- 1 tbsp olive oil
- 2 leeks, sliced
- 4 sage leaves, shredded, or pinch dried
- 85g risotto rice
- small glass white wine
- 200ml hot vegetable stock
- 2-3 rashers streaky bacon
- 3 tbsp grated parmesan

Directions:

1. Heat the oil in a pan, add the leeks and sage and fry for 2 mins until the leeks are starting to soften. Stir in the rice and cook for 1 min, stirring. Add the wine and stock and bring to the boil. Reduce the heat, cover and simmer for 10-12 mins until the rice is tender.
2. Meanwhile, grill the bacon until golden and crisp. Remove the rice from the heat, then stir in 2 tbsp of the Parmesan and freshly ground pepper. Spoon onto a plate, sprinkle with the remaining Parmesan and top with the bacon.

Nutritional Value (Amount per Serving):

Calories: 2112; Fat: 220.32; Carb: 44.79; Protein: 11.17

Grilled Marinated Lamb Cutlets

Prep Time: 5 Mins
Cook Time: 6 Mins   Serves: 2

Ingredients:

- 2 tbsp pomegranate molasses
- juice 1/2 lemon, plus wedges to serve
- 1 tbsp olive oil
- 1 tsp chilli powder
- 4-6 lamb cutlets, depending on size
- 2 tbsp Greek yogurt

Directions:

1. Mix together the pomegranate molasses, lemon juice, olive oil and chilli powder, then toss the cutlets in it. Cover and leave in a cool place for 2-3 hrs.
2. When you are ready, heat the grill to high. Lift the cutlets out of the marinade and scrape what is left into a bowl. Mix the yogurt into the leftover marinade and add 1 tsp salt. Brush some of the mix over the cutlets on both sides and place on the grill plate – make sure it's about 5cm below the grill. Cook for 2-3 mins each side, brushing with additional yogurt mix when turning. The cutlets should be browned and just beginning to scorch. Serve with lemon wedges.

Nutritional Value (Amount per Serving):

Calories: 2041; Fat: 123.72; Carb: 54.59; Protein: 173.15

Provençal Pork Skewers

Prep Time: 10 Mins
Cook Time: 8 Mins   Serves: 4

Ingredients:

- 600g pork fillet
- bunch spring onions
- 2 tsp dried herbes de Provence
- zest and juice 1 lemon
- 1 tbsp clear honey
- 1 tbsp olive oil

Directions:

1. Cut the pork into bite-size chunks and cut

the spring onions into 3cm lengths. In a bowl mix together the herbs, lemon zest and juice, honey, oil and a little seasoning. Add the pork and onions and stir well to coat all the pieces of meat evenly.
2. Thread the meat and onion alternately onto 4 or 8 skewers. Heat grill until hot. Cook the skewers for 6-8 mins, turning occasionally, until browned.

Nutritional Value (Amount per Serving):

Calories: 452; Fat: 29.95; Carb: 6.02; Protein: 37.74

Spiced Lamb With Lemon Herb Quinoa

Prep Time: 15 Mins
Cook Time: 20 Mins   Serves: 4

Ingredients:

- 1 tbsp cumin seed
- 1 garlic clove
- 1/4 tsp red chilli or pinch of chilli flakes
- juice 1 lemon
- 4 tbsp olive oil
- 8 lamb chops
- 250g quinoa
- 5 spring onions, sliced
- small handful coriander
- steamed stem broccoli, to serve

Directions:

1. In a pestle with a mortar crush the cumin seeds then add the garlic clove, chilli and some salt and pepper. Mash to a paste. Stir in the lemon juice and olive oil and pour half the mix over the lamb chops and leave to marinate. Set the other half aside.
2. Rinse the quinoa in cold water then place in a saucepan with twice the volume of water. Place on the heat and bring to the boil then turn down the heat slightly and boil gently for 10 mins. Turn the heat off and stir through the reserved dressing. Cover and leave for another 10 mins.
3. Meanwhile heat a grill to high and cook the lamb for about 3-5 mins on each side or until cooked to your liking. When ready to serve stir the spring onions and coriander through the quinoa and serve with the lamb and steamed stem broccoli dressed in a drizzle more oil.

Nutritional Value (Amount per Serving):

Calories: 693; Fat: 33.56; Carb: 43.59; Protein: 55.56

Chapter 4: Poultry

Buffalo Hunter'S Chicken

Prep Time: 20 Mins
Cook Time: 45 Mins   Serves: 4

Ingredients:

- 4 skinless chicken breasts, around 8oz each
- 200g firm mozzarella, cut unto 8 pieces
- 16 rashers of streaky bacon (dry cured is best to use for this recipe)
- 4 tsp of buffalo seasoning or similar American style seasoning (cajun or bbq will do as well)
- Good quality bbq sauce to brush the chicken (or make your own using the recipe bellow)
- Salt and pepper to season
- or The Home-Made Bbq Sauce
- 400ml of passata   • Pinch salt
- 30ml apple cider vinegar
- 60ml maple syrup   30g of sugar
- 1 tbsp Worcestershire sauce
- 1 tbsp smoked paprika
- 1 tsp chilli powder
- 1 tsp cumin powder
- 1 tsp onion powder
- 1 tsp garlic powder
- Pinch white pepper

Directions:

1. If using ready made bbq sauce, skip to step two. To make the sauce, combine all ingredients in a pan and heat up gently. Simmer for 10 mins until thickened. Use for the recipe and store the remaining sauce in an air tight container in the fridge for up to 1 week.
2. Turn the ninja grill on and preheat on roast function at 160 °C.
3. Butterfly the chickens and gently pound them with a meat mallet.
4. Rub the seasoning in and allow it to soak into the chicken for a couple of minutes.
5. Add two pieces of mozzarella in each chicken and roll tight, then wrap with 4 rashers of back. Repeat for all 4 pieces of chicken.
6. Place the chicken portions in the crisper basket and cook in the grill for 15 mins then brush generously with bbq sauce, change the function of the grill to air crisp and cook for another 5 mins at 200 C until crispy and golden brown. Ensure the chicken has reached safe temperature of 75 °C and if needed cook for another couple of minutes (cooking time will depend on size of portions).
7. Once ready take the chicken out and rest for 5 mins before carving. Serve with a side of your choice.

Nutritional Value (Amount per Serving):

Calories: 318; Fat: 7.88; Carb: 39.69; Protein: 25.08

Air Fryer Chicken Gyro Recipe

Prep Time: 5 Mins
Cook Time: 1 Hr   Serves: 4

Ingredients:

- 1 Kg Chicken Thighs Boneless Skinless
- Pitta Bread
- 1 Large Tomato diced
- 1 Medium Cucumber diced
- Shredded Lettuce optional
- reek Gyro Marinade
- 3 Garlic Cloves
- 1 Tbsp Balsamic Vinegar
- 1 Tbsp Lemon Juice
- 1 Tbsp Extra Virgin Olive Oil
- 2 Tbsp Thick Greek Yoghurt
- 2 Tsp Oregano
- Salt & Pepper
- zatziki Sauce
- 1 Small Lemon juice only
- 1 Tsp Garlic Puree
- 3 Tbsp Greek Yoghurt

Directions:

1. Place your marinade ingredients into a Ziploc bag with your chicken thighs and give them a good mix. Load the Ziploc into a bowl and then place in the fridge overnight.
2. The next day remove the bowl from the fridge and get rid of the Ziploc bag. Using the attachment for the rotisserie load the chicken onto it and then push it down to fit in as much as you can.
3. Then secure the rotisserie into place and air fry for 30 minutes at 180 °C, followed by a further 30 minutes at 160 °C.
4. Whilst the air fryer is rotating make your tzatziki sauce by mixing some of the cucumber you have diced with the rest of the tzatziki sauce ingredients. Then test and if too garlicky balance it out with a little more lemon juice and Greek yoghurt.
5. Also load the rest of the cucumber into a bowl, another with tomato and then get out anything else you plan to serve with it.
6. When the chicken thigh gyros are cooked allow to cool for about 5 minutes.
7. Then remove from the rotisserie and it will be like a big log of chicken pieces and then slice them lengthways into chunks that resemble chicken kebabs you have purchased.
8. Once fully sliced you will have a big collection of gyro chicken meat that you can then make a gyro bowl with or load into pitta breads with your cucumber, tomato, and sauce.

Nutritional Value (Amount per Serving):

Calories: 212; Fat: 2.99; Carb: 19.32; Protein: 27.92

Grilled Chicken With Chilli Sesame Seeds

Prep Time: 10 Mins
Cook Time: 10 Mins   Serves: 2

Ingredients:

- 2 skinless chicken breasts
- 1 tbsp vegetable oil
- 1 1/2tbsp sriracha chilli sauce (see tip below)
- 2 tsp grated ginger
- 2 tbsp clear honey
- 2 tbsp rice vinegar
- 240g pack Tenderstem broccoli
- 1 tbsp sesame seeds ,toasted

Directions:

1. Slice each chicken breast lengthways into 2 thin pieces. Rub with the oil and season on both sides. Heat a grill plate and cook the pieces for 2-3 mins each side.
2. While the chicken is cooking,mix the chilli sauce,ginger,honey and vinegar with a little seasoning in a small bowl. Brush over the chicken as it cooks – wait until it is grilled on one side first before brushing,or it will burn.
3. Blanch the broccoli,divide between the plates and pour over the remaining sauce. Top with the chicken and sesame seeds.

Nutritional Value (Amount per Serving):

Calories: 268; Fat: 11.73; Carb: 22.59; Protein: 20.9

Air Fryer Piri Piri Chicken Legs

Prep Time: 5 Mins
Cook Time: 22 Mins   Serves: 4

Ingredients:

- 4 chicken legs
- 2 tsp Piri Piri spice mix
- 120g Piri Piri marinade sauce (approx)

Directions:

1. Add the spice mix and sauce to the raw chicken legs. Leave them to marinate for

around 30 minutes.
2. Transfer to the crisper basket and cook at 190 °C for 22 minutes.
3. Turn the chicken legs at the halfway mark.
4. The chicken legs are ready when the juices run clear and the internal temperature is 75 °C use a meat thermometer if necessary.

Nutritional Value (Amount per Serving):

Calories: 345; Fat: 11.19; Carb: 4.87; Protein: 52.55

Air Fryer Chicken Breasts

Prep Time: 10 Mins
Cook Time: 20 Mins   Serves: 4

Ingredients:

- 1 chicken breast (increase accordingly)
- 1/2 tbsp olive oil
- 1/2 tsp salt
- 1/2 tsp pepper
- 1/2 tsp garlic powder (or seasoning of your choice)

Directions:

1. Preheat the air fryer at 180 °C.
2. Brush or spray each chicken breast with oil.
3. Season one side (the smooth side) of each chicken breast.
4. Place each chicken breast (smooth side down) in the crisper basket. Season the other side.
5. Set the timer for 10 minutes.
6. After 10 minutes turn the chicken breasts over to allow them to cook on both sides.
7. Check the chicken is cooked all the way through - use a meat thermometer if necessary.
8. Leave the chicken to rest for 5 minutes before serving or slicing.

Nutritional Value (Amount per Serving):

Calories: 143; Fat: 8.42; Carb: 0.82; Protein: 15.29

Air Fryer Chicken Wings

Prep Time: 5 Mins
Cook Time: 25 Mins   Serves: 4

Ingredients:

- 1 kg chicken wings
- 1 tbsp olive oil
- 1/2tsp garlic powder
- 1/2tsp onion powder
- 1/2tsp paprika
- 1/2tsp salt
- 1/2tsp black pepper

Directions:

1. Preheat the air fryer at 180 °C.
2. Prepare the chicken wings by firstly patting them dry with some kitchen roll. The dryer the chicken wings are, the crispier they will come out.
3. Add the wings to a large bowl and cover with the olive oil, tossing them so that they are all covered as much as possible.
4. Add all the seasonings, coating all the wings.
5. Put the chicken wings in the air fryer. Depending on how many wings you are cooking, and the size of your air fryer, you might need to do them in batches. You can also use a rack in your air fryer to fit more in. The key thing is to make sure the wings are not touching each other so that they have room to crisp up.
6. Cook for 20 minutes, turning and shaking 2 or 3 times to ensure they cook evenly.
7. Increase the temperature to 200 °C and cook for a further 5 minutes or until the skin is crispy.
8. Serve with BBQ sauce, Hot Pepper Sauce, Buffalo Sauce

Nutritional Value (Amount per Serving):

Calories: 561; Fat: 35.11; Carb: 9.28; Protein: 49.35

Air Fryer Hunters Chicken

Prep Time: 5 Mins
Cook Time: 25 Mins   Serves: 2

Ingredients:

- 2 chicken breasts (1 chicken breast per person)
- 4 rashers of bacon (1 or 2 per chicken piece)
- 6 tbsp BBQ sauce
- 50g grated cheese (cheddar, mozzarella, gouda or parmesan)

Directions:

1. Place the chicken breasts in the crisper basket at 190 °C and set the timer for 10 minutes. Turn the chicken at the 5-minute mark.
2. After 10 minutes of cooking time, using some tongs or a fork, remove the chicken breasts and wrap each one in one or two rashers of bacon. To keep the rashers in place, you can use a cocktail stick.
3. Return the bacon-wrapped chicken to the basket and cook for a further 10 minutes, again turning halfway.
4. At the end of the cooking time, open the basket and brush the BBQ sauce equally over each chicken breast.
5. Sprinkle the grated cheese over the top of the BBQ sauce.
6. Air fry for a further 2 to 3 minutes or until the cheese has melted and the BBQ sauce is hot.
7. Remove from the air fryer, and remove the cocktail sticks if you used them.
8. Check the chicken is cooked all the way through, either by cutting into one or using a meat thermometer.
9. Serve with your favourite side dish.

Nutritional Value (Amount per Serving):

Calories: 1803; Fat: 118.5; Carb: 3.96; Protein: 169.98

Air Fryer BBQ Chicken Breast

Prep Time: 3 Mins
Cook Time: 20 Mins   Serves: 2

Ingredients:

- 2 chicken breasts 1 per person
- Spray oil
- Salt and pepper
- Smoked paprika
- Garlic salt or garlic powder
- 80 ml BBQ sauce

Directions:

1. Spray your chicken breasts with spray oil.
2. Sprinkle over smoked paprika, garlic salt and season well with salt and pepper too. Alternatively you can mix it all together beforehand and sprinkle on.
3. Turn over and repeat this step again.
4. Lay the chicken in the crisper basket.
5. Cook at 180 °C for 10 minutes.
6. Turn over the chicken breast.
7. Cook at 180 °C for another 8 minutes.
8. Pour over the barbecue sauce; I like to use a silicone pastry brush to ensure even coverage, but you can just use a spoon or whatever you have to hand.
9. Cook at 180 °C for another 2 minutes.
10. Check the internal temperature of the chicken breast (in the thickest part) is a minimum of 74 °C and then remove.
11. You can rest for 5 minutes before you slice and serve. Or just serve up as a whole chicken breast alongside the rest of your dinner.

Nutritional Value (Amount per Serving):

Calories: 477; Fat: 15.95; Carb: 80.18; Protein: 20.21

Chapter 5: Appetizers and Snacks

Grilled Nectarine Burrata Salad

Prep Time: 10 Mins
Cook Time: 10 Mins   Serves: 4

Ingredients:

- 15g unsalted butter
- 2 tbsp caster sugar
- 50g whole pecans
- 3 ripe nectarines, stoned and cut into eighths lengthways
- 4 tbsp extra virgin olive oil, plus extra for brushing
- 2 tbsp balsamic vinegar
- 1 tsp honey
- 2 x 100g balls of burrata or vegetarian alternative
- 70g rocket
- bunch of basil leaves, roughly torn
- pinch of chilli flakes

Directions:

1. Heat the butter and sugar in a small frying pan over a medium heat until the butter has melted. Add the pecans and stir to coat in the buttery sugar. Continue to cook for about 5 mins, stirring until the pecans are crisp and caramelised. Tip out onto a sheet of baking parchment and leave to cool. Once cooled, roughly chop and set aside.
2. Heat the grill plate over a high heat and generously brush the nectarine slices with some olive oil. Grill for 1-2 mins on each side until charred and caramelised. Remove to a serving platter and set aside.
3. Whisk the 4 tbsp olive oil, vinegar and honey together with some seasoning to make a dressing.
4. Nestle the balls of burrata in amongst the nectarines and slice open, then arrange the rocket and basil around them. Drizzle over the dressing, scatter with the pecans and sprinkle with a pinch of chilli flakes to serve.

Nutritional Value (Amount per Serving):

Calories: 308; Fat: 25.46; Carb: 20.52; Protein: 2.6

Grilled Courgette Halloumi Salad With Caper Lemon Dressing

Prep Time: 10 Mins
Cook Time: 20 Mins   Serves: 4

Ingredients:

- 10-12 baby courgettes,halved lengthways
- 1 tbsp olive oil
- 225g block halloumi,thinly sliced (about 16 slices)
- or The Dressing
- 1 long shallot,finely chopped
- 1 red chilli,finely chopped
- 1 garlic clove,crushed
- 1 lemon,zested and juiced
- 2 tbsp capers
- 3 tbsp olive oil

Directions:

1. Put all the dressing ingredients in a bowl with 1 tbsp cold water and season with a pinch of salt. Mix together and set aside.
2. Put the courgettes in a large bowl and drizzle with the oil. Add a pinch of salt, then toss.
3. Heat the grill plate to high and add the courgettes,cut-side down (it's best to do this in batches). Cook for 4-5 mins until char marks appear and the flesh softens, then flip over and cook for another 3 mins. Remove to a shallow bowl and cover with foil to keep warm.
4. Meanwhile,heat a separate large non-stick frying pan and add the halloumi. Cook for a few minutes until golden on both sides.
5. Arrange the courgettes and halloumi on a large plate or platter,then spoon over the dressing.

Nutritional Value (Amount per Serving):

Calories: 535; Fat: 36.72; Carb: 39.65; Protein: 12.55

Grilled Peach, Chicken Feta Salad

Prep Time: 10 Mins
Cook Time: 12 Mins   Serves: 4

Ingredients:

- 400g pack mini chicken fillet
- 3 tbsp olive oil
- 4 ripe peaches ,stoned and cut into quarters
- 4 tsp sherry vinegar
- 1 tbsp clear honey
- 1 red chilli ,finely chopped
- 110g bag herb salad
- 100g feta cheese ,crumbled

Directions:

1. Heat the grill plate. Toss the chicken in 1/2tbsp of the oil,and season. Cook for 3-4 mins on each side or until cooked through. Pop on a plate to rest.
2. Next toss the peach slices in 1/2tbsp oil and some ground black pepper. Grill on their cut sides for 1-2 mins each side.
3. Mix the remaining olive oil,vinegar,honey and chilli. Toss with the salad leaves. Arrange the chicken and nectarine slices on top and scatter with the feta. Drizzle with the resting juices from the chicken and eat straight away.

Nutritional Value (Amount per Serving):

Calories: 547; Fat: 38.83; Carb: 26.03; Protein: 24.64

Spiced Grilled Pineapple With Maple Sesame Brittle

Prep Time: 15 Mins
Cook Time: 20 Mins   Serves: 4

Ingredients:

- 2 limes ,zested and juiced
- pinch ground ginger
- pinch mixed spice
- 3 tbsp maple syrup
- 1 medium ripe pineapple
- vegetable oil ,for grilling
- small handful Thai basil or mint leaves and thick Greek yogurt or frozen yogurt,to serve
- or The Brittle

- 25g maple syrup
- 100g caster sugar
- 100g butter
- 50g sesame seeds
- 1/2tsp sea salt flakes

Directions:

1. To make the brittle, line a heavy baking tray with parchment, and put the maple syrup, sugar, butter and 25ml water in a heavy-based saucepan. Stir until the sugar has melted, then leave to bubble on a medium heat for 15 mins or until dark golden brown. Stir in the sesame seeds and sea salt flakes, and stir briefly before pouring onto the lined tray. Working carefully so you don't touch the sugar and burn yourself, spread out into a thin layer. Leave to cool and harden.
2. Mix the lime juice and most of the lime zest with the ground ginger, mixed spice and maple syrup. Top and tail the pineapple, cut away the skin and any black marks from the flesh, then cut into 1cm slices. Toss with the lime and maple mix, then leave for at least 30 mins to marinate.
3. Wait until the embers are low on a barbecue (the ideal time is after you've cooked a main) or heat the grill plate to hot. Lightly oil the grill bars or griddle pan to prevent the fruit from sticking, and grill the pineapple for 1-2 mins on each side until golden and lightly charred. Cut into bite-sized shards, then transfer to a platter while you cook the rest.
4. Finely slice the larger basil or mint leaves and keep the smaller leaves whole. Bash the brittle into pieces, and serve scattered over the charred pineapple with the herbs and a drizzle of the marinade. Scatter the remaining lime zest over the yogurt or frozen yogurt and serve on the side.

Nutritional Value (Amount per Serving):

Calories: 602; Fat: 36.17; Carb: 46.03; Protein: 28.16

Moroccan Aubergine Chickpea Salad

Prep Time: 15 Mins
Cook Time: 20 Mins   Serves: 4 – 6

Ingredients:

- 2 aubergines
- 2-3 tbsp olive oil
- 400g can chickpeas
- good bunch fresh coriander, roughly chopped
- 1 red onion, finely chopped
- or The Dressing
- 1 tsp each paprika and ground cumin

- 1 tsp clear honey
- 1 lemon, juice only
- 4 tbsp olive oil

Directions:

1. Thickly slice the aubergines and arrange over a grill plate. Brush lightly with oil, sprinkle with salt and pepper, then grill until browned. Turn them over, brush and season again then cook until tender, about 8-10 mins in total. Remove from the grill and cut each slice into quarters.
2. Drain and rinse the chickpeas, then tip into a bowl with the aubergine, coriander and red onion. Mix the dressing ingredients in a screw-top jar, shake well, then use to dress the salad.

Nutritional Value (Amount per Serving):

Calories: 357; Fat: 21.45; Carb: 37.13; Protein: 8.38

Grilled Aubergine Tomato Salad

Prep Time: 15 Mins
Cook Time: 10 Mins   Serves: 6-10

Ingredients:

- 1 aubergine, thinly sliced
- 4 vine tomatoes, roughly chopped
- 1 garlic clove, crushed
- 1 red chilli, diced
- 2 tbsp olive oil, plus a little for brushing
- 2 tbsp red wine vinegar
- 1 bunch basil, roughly chopped

Directions:

1. Heat the grill plate. Brush sliced aubergine with olive oil, then grill for 3 mins on each side. Put in a bowl and cover with cling film for 5 mins.
2. Meanwhile, mix chopped tomatoes with the garlic clove, red chilli, olive oil and red wine vinegar and allow to stand for 10 mins. Lay the aubergine on a platter, pour over the tomatoes with their juices and finish with basil.

Nutritional Value (Amount per Serving):

Calories: 94; Fat: 7.4; Carb: 5.03; Protein: 3

Grilled Tuna With Parsley Salad

Prep Time: 15 Mins
Cook Time: 2 Mins   Serves: 2

Ingredients:

- 2 line-caught yellowfin tuna steaks ,about 140g/5oz each
- 1 tbsp olive oil
- 2 lemons wedges
- or The Parsley Salad
- 2 handfuls (50g/2oz) flat-leaf parsley ,very roughly chopped
- 2 shallots ,finely sliced
- 1 tbsp capers ,roughly chopped
- small handful green olives ,stoned and roughly chopped
- 6 tbsp olive oil
- 1 tbsp Dijon mustard
- juice of half a lemon

Directions:

1. First make up the parsley salad by mixing all the ingredients together and stirring until completely combined. Set aside while you cook the tuna.
2. Heat the grill plate until practically smoking. Rub the tuna with the olive oil and season with salt and pepper. Grill the tuna steaks for 1 min on each side,turning them 90 degrees after 30 secs if you want criss-cross patterns. This will give you tuna that is medium-rare,but if you like it well-cooked give it a few more mins on each side. It's important not to move the fish around the pan before it's seared as it will stick and break up. The steak will release itself from the pan once it's ready to be turned.
3. Serve each steak with half the salad,a lemon wedge for squeezing over and a few new potatoes,if you like.

Nutritional Value (Amount per Serving):

Calories: 470; Fat: 48.56; Carb: 10.37; Protein: 2.91

Chapter 6: Fish and Seafood

Grilled Mackerel With Escalivada Toasts

Prep Time: 15 Mins
Cook Time: 30 Mins			Serves: 4

Ingredients:

- or The Escalivada
- 3 very large or 4 medium peppers a mix of colours
- 1 red onion ,halved and thinly sliced
- 3 tbsp extra virgin olive oil
- 2 medium aubergines
- zest 1 lemon ,juice of
- 1 rosemary sprig,finely chopped
- 2 tbsp small capers ,drained
- small pack flat-leaf parsley ,roughly chopped
- or The Fish And Toasts
- 2 rosemary sprigs,finely chopped
- 3 garlic cloves ,crushed
- 3 tbsp extra virgin olive oil ,plus extra to serve (optional)
- 1 large olive ciabatta ,cut into 8 slices
- 1/4 tsp chilli flakes or hot paprika
- 4 mackerel fillets,pin-boned and cut in half if large (or 8 butterflied sardines)

Directions:

1. Heat the grill as hot as it will go. Line the grill plate. Using a potato peeler, remove most of the skin from the peppers,then remove the seeds and slice into 1cm strips. Toss with the onion and 1 tbsp oil,then grill for 15 mins,stirring halfway,until soft and charring here and there.
2. Cut the aubergines into 1cm half moons and brush sparingly with 2 tbsp oil. Lay the slices over the peppers,season well,then grill for 5 mins until golden. Turn the aubergines over,scatter with the lemon zest and rosemary,then grill for 5 mins more until golden and soft in places. Stir the capers and the lemon juice into the vegetables. Season and set aside. Make and chill up to 3 days ahead; the flavours will intensify as it matures. Make sure you serve it just warm,with the parsley folded through it.
3. For the toasts and fish,mix the rosemary,crushed garlic,oil and some seasoning. Brush half of this over one side of the ciabatta slices. Mix the chilli into the remainder,then brush over the fish and let it marinate for anything from 5 mins to 1 hr in the fridge. Grill the fish,skin-side up (or barbecue skin-side down),for 4-5 mins,depending on the thickness of flesh,until just cooked through and the

skin is crisp. Grill the bread until sizzling and golden. Top the toasts with the escalivada, followed by the fish, and serve with another drizzle oil, if you like.

Nutritional Value (Amount per Serving):

Calories: 647; Fat: 19.84; Carb: 23.36; Protein: 92.21

Grilled Miso Salmon With Rice Noodles

Prep Time: 10 Mins
Cook Time: 20 Mins - 25 Mins
Serves: 4

Ingredients:

- 4 salmon fillets ,about 140g each
- sunflower oil ,for greasing
- or The Miso Glaze
- 2 tsp brown miso paste
- 2 tsp balsamic vinegar
- 2 tsp soy sauce
- 1 tsp Spanish smoked paprika
- or The Noodles
- 200g dried rice noodles
- 3 tbsp sunflower oil
- 3 garlic cloves ,finely grated
- 25g ginger ,finely grated
- 8 spring onions ,sliced
- 2 medium red chillies ,thinly sliced
- 100g beansprouts
- small pack of coriander ,chopped
- 1 tbsp fish sauce

Directions:

1. Boil the noodles for 3 mins in a large pan, drain and rinse under cold water through a sieve and set aside to drain completely.
2. Heat the grill to high. Mix together the miso paste, balsamic vinegar, soy sauce and paprika to make the miso glaze and brush over the salmon fillets with a pastry brush. Lay the salmon skin side down on a greased grill plate and grill for 6-8 mins until just cooked through.
3. Heat the oil in a wok and stir-fry the garlic, ginger, spring onions and chillies for a couple of mins until soft, then add the cooked noodles, beansprouts and coriander. Toss everything together until well combined and turn off the heat. To finish, stir the fish sauce into the stir-fried vegetables and noodles, then pile onto plates, topping with the salmon.

Nutritional Value (Amount per Serving):

Calories: 467; Fat: 23.16; Carb: 51.81; Protein: 13.47

Grilled Salmon Tacos With Chipotle Lime Yogurt

Prep Time: 15 Mins
Cook Time: 10 Mins   Serves: 4

Ingredients:

- 1 tsp garlic salt
- 2 tbsp smoked paprika
- good pinch of sugar
- 500g salmon fillet
- 200ml fat-free yogurt
- 1 tbsp chipotle paste or hot chilli sauce
- juice 1 lime
- o Serve
- 8 small soft flour tortillas ,warmed
- 1/4 small green cabbage ,finely shredded
- small bunch coriander ,picked into sprigs
- few pickled jalapeno chillies ,sliced
- lime wedges,to serve
- hot chilli sauce to serve,(optional)

Directions:

1. Rub the garlic salt,paprika,sugar and some seasoning into the flesh of the salmon fillet. Heat grill to high.
2. Mix the yogurt,chipotle paste or hot sauce and lime juice together in a bowl with some seasoning,and set aside. Place the salmon on a grill plate lined with foil and grill,skin-side down,for 7-8 mins until cooked through. Remove from the grill and carefully peel off and discard the skin.
3. Flake the salmon into large chunks and serve with the warmed tortillas,chipotle yogurt,shredded cabbage,coriander,jalape os and lime wedges. Add a shake of hot sauce,if you like it spicy.

Nutritional Value (Amount per Serving):

Calories: 558; Fat: 15.1; Carb: 67.98; Protein: 36.4

Grilled Bass With Sauce Vierge

Prep Time: 20 Mins
Cook Time: 10 Mins   Serves: 4

Ingredients:

- 50g butter ,melted
- 4 sea bass fillets
- or The Sauce
- 100g cherry tomatoes ,finely chopped
- 2 tsp small capers
- juice of 1/2 lemon
- 1 shallot ,finely chopped
- 100ml extra-virgin olive oil
- handful torn basil leaves and chopped chives, to garnish

Directions:

1. Line a grill plate with foil and brush lightly with butter. Brush the fish on both sides with butter and season. Lay on the foil, skin-side up.
2. Put the tomatoes and shallot in a pan with the capers, lemon juice and oil, and season.
3. Grill the bass for 5-7 mins under a hot grill until just cooked and the skin is starting to brown. Meanwhile, warm the sauce through for 2 mins, then stir in some of the torn basil leaves. Lift the bass onto warmed plates using a fish slice and spoon the sauce around. Serve with steamed new potatoes or small baked potatoes, and add the remaining basil and chives.

Nutritional Value (Amount per Serving):

Calories: 350; Fat: 25.62; Carb: 5.09; Protein: 24.44

Grilled Mackerel Fillets

Prep Time: 5 Mins
Cook Time: 10 Mins   Serves: 2

Ingredients:

- 2 large mackerel fillets
- or The Marinade
- 2 tbsp soy sauce
- 1 tbsp honey
- 1 tsp ground ginger
- 1 garlic clove, crushed to a purée

- 1 tbsp saké or dry sherry
- 1 tsp chilli flakes
- or The Salad
- 2 tsp sesame oil
- 80g Asian-style salad mix (pea shoots, purple radish and coriander)
- 1/2 lime, juiced
- 1 tsp soy sauce
- 1 tsp honey
- 1 tsp sweet chilli sauce

Directions:

1. Mix all the marinade ingredients, then pour over the fish. Set aside for 20 mins.
2. For the salad, combine the sesame oil, lime juice, soy, honey and sweet chilli to make a dressing, then toss with the leaves.
3. Grill the marinated mackerel under a hot grill for 5 mins, basting two or three times with any excess marinade, until the flesh begins to flake. Slice and serve with the dressed salad leaves.

Nutritional Value (Amount per Serving):

Calories: 973; Fat: 35.63; Carb: 26.49; Protein: 133.08

Grilled Thai Salmon

Prep Time: 5 Mins
Cook Time: 10 Mins   Serves: 4

Ingredients:

- 4 x 140g/5oz salmon fillets
- 2 tsp sunflower oil
- small knob of root ginger, peeled and grated
- 1 mild red chilli, finely sliced (deseed if you want less heat)
- bunch spring onions, finely sliced
- 1 1/2 tbsp sweet soy sauce
- 1/4 tsp sugar
- 1 x 20g pack coriander, leaves only chopped

Directions:

1. Heat grill to high. Place the fish in a shallow baking dish, then grill for 4-5 mins until cooked through, but still a little pink in the centre. Cover and set aside.
2. Heat a wok, add the oil, then stir-fry the ginger, chilli and spring onions for 2-3 mins. Stir in the soy, sugar and a splash of water, then take off the heat. Throw in the coriander and serve immediately with the salmon. Delicious with rice or noodles.

Nutritional Value (Amount per Serving):

Calories: 86; Fat: 4.74; Carb: 1.64; Protein: 9.57

Grilled Lobster Tails With Lemon Herb Butter

Prep Time: 20 Mins
Cook Time: 10 Mins   Serves: 4

Ingredients:

- 4 lobster tails, defrosted if frozen
- lemon wedges, to serve
- or The Butter
- 125g butter, softened
- 1 garlic clove, crushed
- handful parsley leaves, finely chopped, plus extra to serve
- 1 tsp Dijon mustard
- small pinch chilli powder, optional
- 1 lemon, juiced

Directions:

1. Make the butter by mixing together all the ingredients, then season and set aside. Can be made two days ahead. Remove from the fridge to soften before using.
2. Use kitchen scissors to cut along the tops of the lobster shells, then flip the tails over and crack the ribs of the shell. Use your fingers to open the shell and loosen the meat keeping it attached at the base and pull it half out. Use a knife to cut along the top of the tail without cutting all the way through and remove the vein if you see one. Sit the tail in a shallow roasting tray and add some butter to each one. Tails can be prepared a few hours ahead and chilled.
3. Heat the grill to high, then grill the lobster tails for 10 mins until cooked through. Put them on plates and drizzle with the butter from the pan, or pour the butter into a ramekin and put it in the middle of the table for dipping the lobster meat in. Serve with lemon wedges and scatter with extra parsley, if you like.

Nutritional Value (Amount per Serving):

Calories: 278; Fat: 27.43; Carb: 8.52; Protein: 1.41

Jamaican Beer Grilled Fish

Prep Time: 15 Mins
Cook Time: 15 Mins   Serves: 4

Ingredients:

- 2 medium red snappers or whole bream, gutted, scaled and cleaned
- 1 tbsp onion powder
- 2 tsp sweet smoked paprika
- pinch dried thyme
- 100ml Jamaican beer (we used Red Stripe), plus extra to baste
- 2 limes, 1 sliced, 1 cut into wedges

Directions:

1. Make a few slashes in the flesh on either side of the fish with a sharp knife. Mix the onion powder, paprika, thyme and some seasoning with the beer. Pour over the fish and rub into the slashes and cavity. Place the lime slices inside the fishes' bellies, cover with cling film and leave to marinate in the fridge for 1 hr.
2. Heat the grill to medium-high. Place the fish on the plate and grill for 15-20 mins, depending on the size, turning halfway through. Baste the fish with a little beer as it cooks. Serve with lime wedges to squeeze over.

Nutritional Value (Amount per Serving):

Calories: 46; Fat: 1.43; Carb: 6.53; Protein: 2.86

Chapter 7: Desserts

Air Fryer Apricot And Raisin Cake

Prep Time: 10 Mins
Cook Time: 12 Mins   Serves: 8

Ingredients:

- 75g dried apricots,
- 4 tbsp orange juice
- 75g self-raising flour,
- 40 g Sugar
- 1 egg
- 75g Raisins

Directions:

1. Preheat air fryer to 160 °C.
2. In a blender or food processor blend the dried apricots and juice until they are smooth.
3. In a separate bowl, mix together the sugar and flour.
4. Beat the egg. Add it to the flour and sugar. Mix together.
5. Add the apricot puree and raisins. Combine together.
6. Spray an air fryer safe baking tin with a little oil. Transfer the mixture over and level off.
7. Cook in the air fryer for 12 minutes, check it at 10 minutes. Use a metal skewer to see if it is done. If need be, return the cake to the air fryer to cook for a few more minutes to brown up.
8. Allow to cool before removing from the baking tin and slicing up.

Nutritional Value (Amount per Serving):

Calories: 95; Fat: 1.37; Carb: 18.8; Protein: 2.58

Air Fryer Chocolate Brownies

Prep Time: 10 Mins
Cook Time: 20-25 Mins   Serves: 16

Ingredients:

- Air fryer
- Air fryer baking tin
- 1 pack brownie mix
- 3 Tablespoons vegetable oil
- 75ml water
- 1 medium egg

64 | Air Fryer Cookbook

Directions:

1. Pour the brownie mix into a bowl then add the water, vegetable oil and egg. Mix it thoroughly and ensure the mixture doesn't have any lumps.
2. Grease the air fryer baking tin and spread the mixture around to get a consistent level throughout.
3. Set the air fryer to 160 °C and let the brownies cook for 20-25 minutes. Stick a knife into the brownie and if it comes out almost clean the brownies should be finished.
4. Allow to cool off then slice up into squares and enjoy your air fried brownies.

Nutritional Value (Amount per Serving):

Calories: 204; Fat: 9.44; Carb: 29.74; Protein: 2.13

Air Fryer Peanut Butter Cookies

Prep Time: 4 Mins
Cook Time: 4 Mins   Serves: 20

Ingredients:

- 250 g smooth peanut butter
- 250 g white caster sugar
- 1 egg

Directions:

1. Mix together the ingredients until you've got a smooth consistency. Try not to overwork the mixture.
2. Line your crisper basket with baking paper.
   You can use reusable baking paper if you have this instead.
3. (If you're going to make multiple batches like I do then you'll want to measure the baking paper before you heat up the air fryer, cut your paper and then you'll have it all to hand ready to line with the cookie dough before placing into the basket carefully to avoid burning yourself).
4. Place walnut sized balls of the dough on to the baking paper.
5. Press down lightly with a fork or spoon, depending on whether you want the little cut indentations or not.
6. Cook at 200 °C for 4 minutes. Check at the 2 minute mark just to ensure the dough balls haven't moved together as air flow can be very strong in some air fryer models.
7. You want to remove these when they are just lightly golden brown to avoid burning them.
8. Depending on your air fryer model you may want to add another 1-2 minutes of

cook time. I use the OL750UK and this heats up VERY fast!

9. Remove from the crisper basket and leave to cool on a wire rack. I like to just remove the parchment paper using a spatula, carefully, and then individually transfer to the wire rack from there. This works great when cooking multiple batches, which I usually am.

Nutritional Value (Amount per Serving):

Calories: 109; Fat: 8.58; Carb: 6.79; Protein: 2.15

Air Fryer Dessert Pizza

Prep Time: 5 Mins
Cook Time: 5 Mins   Serves: 8

Ingredients:

- 1 pizza base
- 150 ml chocolate spread
- 150 g strawberries
- Mint to garnish

Directions:

1. Oil the air fryer basket lightly.
2. Take your pizza base, or rolled out pizza dough, and place it into the lightly oiled crisper basket.
3. Cook this undressed pizza base at 200 °C for 5 minutes until it is lightly cooked.
4. While this is cooking wipe over and remove the tops from your strawberries. Then slice your strawberries either in half or into thinner slices to lay across the cooked base.
5. Leave to cool slightly for a few minutes on a cooling rack.
6. Spread across the chocolate spread. The residual heat from the base will melt this and make it easier to spread.
7. Add your strawberries and spread across in a nice pattern.
8. Add a mint garnish.
9. Slice and serve.
10. See above for more topping suggestions.

Nutritional Value (Amount per Serving):

Calories: 3116; Fat: 167.06; Carb: 356.4; Protein: 42.65

Air Fryer Cookies

Prep Time: 10 Mins
Cook Time: 5 Mins   Serves: 24

Ingredients:

- Cookie dough recipe:
- 135 g salted butter
- 70 g light brown sugar
- 70 g sugar
- 10 ml vanilla extract
- 1 medium egg
- 225 g plain flour
- 1/2 tsp bicarbonate of soda
- pinch of salt
- 175 g chocolate chunks or chips

Directions:

1. Beat the butter and both sugars together in a bowl.
2. Once mixed add the egg and vanilla extract.
3. In a separate bowl combine together the flour, bicarbonate of soda, salt and chocolate chunks (or chips!).
4. Add the dry ingredients to the wet ingredients and mix until combined well.
5. Roll the dough into a long sausage shape and chill for a minimum of 1 hour ideally. This will help to make for a more delicious chewy cookie. On occasion I've left the dough overnight and the cookies are even better!
6. If you're in a hurry you could skip the chilling, but I really feel it adds to the overall texture of the cookies so try to make time!
7. Roll out your cookie dough. I've experimented with balls, lightly press down with a fork, moulding cookie shapes and just cutting off a little slab from the chilled dough and they all take very similar time to cook, with similar results, so just be lazy and cut a slab off if you fancy!
8. Pre-heat your air fryer to 180c for 1-2 minutes if required.
9. Cut a piece of parchment paper to fit the bottom of your air fryer. Without this the cookie dough may mould to the shape of the bottom of your basket and it will be a nightmare to get it out without it breaking up!
10. I lightly sprayed the parchment paper with 1 calorie spray oil but I think you could get away with skipping this step if you don't have any in.
11. Cook for 5 minutes.
12. Transfer to a wire cooling rack, still on the parchment paper, and leave to cook for 5 minutes.

13. Gently peel back the parchment paper and you can enjoy your cookies while they are still warm, or they'll keep for 2-3 days in an airtight container.

Nutritional Value (Amount per Serving):

Calories: 174; Fat: 6.98; Carb: 19.54; Protein: 1.6

Air Fryer Chocolate Chip Cookies

Prep Time: 10 Mins
Cook Time: 35 Mins   Serves: 1

Ingredients:

- 115 g butter, melted
- 55 g brown sugar
- 50 g caster sugar
- 1 large egg
- 1 tsp. pure vanilla extract
- 185 g plain flour
- 1/2 tsp. bicarbonate of soda
- 1/2 tsp. salt
- 120 g chocolate chips
- 35 g chopped walnuts

Directions:

1. In a medium bowl whisk together melted butter and sugars. Add egg and vanilla and whisk until incorporated. Add flour, bicarbonate of soda, and salt and stir until just combined.
2. Place a small piece of parchment in the basket of the air fryer, making sure there is still room around the edges to allow air flow. Working in batches, use a large cookie scoop, about 3 tablespoons, and scoop dough onto parchment, leaving 5cm between each cookie, press to flatten slightly.
3. Bake in air fryer at 180 °C for 8 minutes. Cookies will be golden and slightly soft. Let cool 5 minutes before serving.

Nutritional Value (Amount per Serving):

Calories: 2537; Fat: 123.78; Carb: 330.06; Protein: 30.64

Air Fryer Brownies

Prep Time: 5 Mins
Cook Time: 30 Mins   Serves: 2

Ingredients:

- 100 g caster sugar
- 40 g cocoa powder
- 30 g plain flour
- 1/4 tsp. baking powder
- Pinch salt
- 60 g butter, melted and cooled slightly
- 1 large egg

Directions:

1. Grease a 15cm round cake pan with cooking spray. In a medium bowl, whisk to combine sugar, cocoa powder, flour, baking powder, and salt.
2. In a small bowl, whisk melted butter and egg until combined. Add wet ingredients to dry ingredients and stir until combined.
3. Transfer brownie batter to prepared cake pan and smooth top. Cook in air fryer at 180 °C for 16-18 minutes. Let cool 10 minutes before slicing.

Nutritional Value (Amount per Serving):

Calories: 931; Fat: 57; Carb: 92.15; Protein: 14.37

Air Fryer Cinnamon Rolls

Prep Time: 5 Mins
Cook Time: 25 Mins   Serves: 6

Ingredients:

- or The Rolls
- 2 tbsp. melted butter, plus more for brushing
- 75 g packed brown sugar
- 1/2 tsp. ground cinnamon
- Salt
- Plain flour, for surface
- 225 g ready rolled pizza dough
- or The Glaze
- 50 g cream cheese, softened
- 65 g icing sugar
- 1 tbsp. whole milk, plus more if needed

Directions:

1. Make rolls: Line bottom of air fryer with parchment paper and brush with butter. In a medium bowl, combine butter, brown sugar, cinnamon, and a large pinch of salt until smooth and fluffy.
2. On a lightly floured surface, roll out dough in one piece. Pinch seams together and fold in half. Roll into a 22-cm x 18-cm (9"-x-7") rectangle. Spread butter mixture over dough, leaving 1.5-cm border. Starting at a long edge, roll up dough, then cut crosswise into 6 pieces.
3. Arrange pieces in prepared air fryer, cut-side up, spaced evenly.
4. Set air fryer to 180 °C, and cook until golden and cooked through, about 10 minutes.
5. Make the glaze: In a medium bowl, Whisk cream cheese, icing sugar, and milk together. Add more milk by the teaspoonful, if necessary, to thin glaze.
6. Spread glaze over warm cinnamon rolls and serve.

Nutritional Value (Amount per Serving):

Calories: 340; Fat: 9.88; Carb: 43.07; Protein: 20.17

Air Fryer French Toast Sticks

Prep Time: 5 Mins
Cook Time: 30 Mins   Serves: 6

Ingredients:

- 2 large eggs
- 80 ml double cream
- 80 ml whole milk
- 3 tbsp. caster sugar
- 1/4 tsp. ground cinnamon
- 1/2 tsp. vanilla extract
- Salt
- 6 thick slices white loaf or brioche, each slice cut into thirds
- Maple syrup, for serving

Directions:

1. Beat eggs, cream, milk, sugar, cinnamon, vanilla, and a pinch of salt in a large shallow baking dish. Add bread, turn to coat a few times.
2. Arrange french toast in basket of air fryer, working in batches as necessary to not overcrowd basket. Set air fryer to 190 °C and cook until golden, about 8 minutes, tossing halfway through.
3. Serve toast warm, drizzled with maple syrup.

Nutritional Value (Amount per Serving):

Calories: 1377; Fat: 95.39; Carb: 78.32; Protein: 57.27

CONCLUSION

Given its cooking surface, the Ninja Foodi Max Pro Health Grill, Flat Plate, and Air Fryer is an extremely practical kitchen appliance. In addition to offering the same great cooking possibilities as the earlier AG301UK, it also adds temperature-probe controlled cooking and open-lid cooking (flat plate and grill). It's a great pick if you'll use all of its cooking modes.

APPENDIX RECIPE INDEX

A

Air Fryer Chickpeas..19
Air Fryer Breakfast Potatoes...................................20
Air Fryer Jacket Potato..21
Air Fryer Beef Wellington.......................................29
Air Fryer Roast Beef..31
Air Fryer Chicken Gyro Recipe................................42
Air Fryer Piri Piri Chicken Legs................................43
Air Fryer Chicken Breasts..44
Air Fryer Chicken Wings..45
Air Fryer Hunters Chicken.......................................46
Air Fryer BBQ Chicken Breast..................................47
Air Fryer Apricot And Raisin Cake...........................64
Air Fryer Chocolate Brownies..................................64
Air Fryer Peanut Butter Cookies..............................65
Air Fryer Dessert Pizza..66
Air Fryer Cookies...67
Air Fryer Chocolate Chip Cookies............................68
Air Fryer Brownies...69
Air Fryer Cinnamon Rolls..69
Air Fryer French Toast Sticks...................................70

B

Breakfast Muffin..18
Buffalo Hunter'S Chicken..41

C

Cheesy French Toast With Ham Grilled Vine Tomatoes..17
Crispy Grilled Feta With Saucy Butter Beans.........23

D
E
F
G

Grilled Pesto Tomatoes on Toast.............................16
Grilled Courgette,Bean Cheese Quesadilla.............24
Grilled Aubergines With Spicy Chickpeas Walnut Sauce..25
Grilled Mediterranean Veg With Bean Mash..........26
Grilled Steak Topped With Ceps..............................32
Grilled Pork With Lemon Thyme Barley.................33
Grilled Steak Salad With Horseradish Dressing......34
Grilled Saigon Pork Rib..35
Grilled Marinated Lamb Cutlets..............................38
Grilled Chicken With Chilli Sesame Seeds..............43
Grilled Nectarine Burrata Salad...............................49
Grilled Courgette Halloumi Salad With Caper Lemon Dressing..50
Grilled Peach,Chicken Feta Salad............................51
Grilled Aubergine Tomato Salad..............................53
Grilled Tuna With Parsley Salad..............................54
Grilled Mackerel With Escalivada Toasts.................56
Grilled Miso Salmon With Rice Noodles.................57
Grilled Salmon Tacos With Chipotle Lime Yogurt..58
Grilled Bass With Sauce Vierge................................59
Grilled Mackerel Fillets..59
Grilled Thai Salmon..60
Grilled Lobster Tails With Lemon Herb Butter.......61

H

Hoisin Hot Dogs...18
Homemade Air Fryer Fishcakes................................30

I
J

Jamaican Beer Grilled Fish......................................62

K
L

Leek Sage Risotto With Grilled Crisp Bacon..........37

M

Moroccan Aubergine Chickpea Salad......................52

N
O
P

Pork Chop Melts..35
Provençal Pork Skewers...38

Q

Quinoa Salad With Grilled Halloumi.......................23

R
S

Spiced Flat Breads...16
Stuffed Grilled Vegetable Bites................................27
Sesame Beef Skewers With Cucumber Salad..........36
Spiced Lamb With Lemon Herb Quinoa.................39
Spiced Grilled Pineapple With Maple Sesame Brittle51

Printed in Great Britain
by Amazon